Arts Council of Great Britain

EDVARD MUNCH

1863–1944

Haus der Kunst, Munich
6 October – 16 December 1973

Hayward Gallery, London
12 January – 3 March 1974

Musée National d'Art Moderne, Paris
22 March – 12 May 1974

Catalogue designed by Graham Johnson/Lund Humphries
and printed in Great Britain by Lund Humphries, London and Bradford

This exhibition has been organised by the Arts Council of Great Britain in association with the Haus der Kunst, Munich, and the Réunion des Musées Nationaux, France

Lenders to the exhibition

Bergen, Rasmus Meyer Collection
Bergen, Billedgalleri
Annie Bergh, Oslo
Hamburg, Kunsthalle
Hanover, Niedersächsisches Landesmuseum, Städtische Galerie
Helsinki, Ateneumim Taidemuseo
Carl H. Hudtwalcker
O. Hudtwalcker, Barcelona
F. Lorentzen
Norske Selskab, Oslo
Oslo, National Gallery
Oslo, Munch Museum
Prague, Národní Galerie v Praze
Schwarz-von Spreckelsen, Basel
Stockholm, Moderna Museet
Stockholm, Thielska Galleriet
Stuttgart, Staatsgalerie – Graphische Sammlung
Trondheim, Tröndelag Kunstgalleri
Wuppertal, Von der Heydt-Museum
Zürich, Kunsthaus

Foreword

To make this exhibition possible Norway has allowed a great number of Edvard Munch's finest works to be absent from her museums. We most warmly appreciate this generosity. We are specially indebted to the National Gallery, Oslo, the Munch Museum, Oslo, and the Municipal Collections in Bergen. We are most grateful to all other lenders from public and private collections who have responded nobly to requests for loans; they are listed on the facing page.

Our special thanks are due to Mr Pål Hougen, Director of the Munch Museum, who has undertaken the main task of selecting and organising the exhibition, and to Mr Knut Berg, Director of the National Gallery, who has provided an introductory essay. Professor Heiberg and his colleagues on the Honorary Committee of the exhibition have rendered the most valuable assistance to the project. Mr P. A. Ade of the Haus der Kunst, Munich has coordinated with great patience and skill the practical details of the exhibition.

Lord Clark most kindly agreed to our pressing request that he should write on the art of Munch for this catalogue. We are delighted to have his masterly and illuminating contribution.

Robin Campbell *Director of Art*
Norbert Lynton *Director of Exhibitions*
Arts Council of Great Britain

Edvard Munch
by Kenneth Clark

Fifty years ago English taste was dominated by an effort to assimilate Cézanne and what was known as 'post-impressionist' painting. No one dreamt of looking for art outside of Paris. The accepted critical dogma was that painting should affect us by means of pure visual sensations related to each other by a classical sense of design. The content of a picture was supposed to be immaterial, but if it contained any reference to human relationships it was condemned as 'literary'.

In such a climate of opinions it is not surprising that Edvard Munch should have been overlooked or condemned, for no painter had based his art more completely on an intense concern for human relationships. He said that 'art is crystallisation', which expresses very well the mysterious process by which fluid ideas and associations take on an apparently inevitable form. But the ideas that crystallised in his mind were inspired by a limited number of emotional experiences – fear, jealousy, loneliness, nameless longings, the misery of death and the consequences of physical passion. For all these he found images so compelling, so completely 'crystallised', that they achieved the character of obsessive symbols. Like all visonary artists – Blake and El Greco are obvious examples – these moments of form-creating insight came to him rather rarely, and the images they deposited could never be dislodged. One of them, *The Sick Child*, which seems to have been his first fully realised moment of vision, he continued to reproduce with minor variations throughout his life. Some, like the two lonely people by the shore, came to him complete and were never varied. Others, like the couple embracing, he worked on for years, concentrating, simplifying, till the final result is almost an abstraction.

This need to reduce his most strongly felt moments of vision to pictorial essences was, I believe, partly responsible for his devotion to the media of wood-cut and lithography, not only because they could allow a simplification unnatural in oil paint, but because the blocks could be endlessly reworked and reprinted. Munch's graphic work is a repertoire of his obsessive images, and many people may find it the most convincing part of his œuvre. But Munch was also a born painter. Although he deliberately renounced *jolie matière* in order to present his visions more starkly, he could paint, if he chose, with the delicacy of a Vuillard.

All his work makes it evident that Munch was a deeply neurotic man. He was exceptionally handsome and never married. No doubt he had some strange experiences with the opposite sex, and he developed an almost Strindbergian view of woman as sorceress or vampire. Strindberg himself wrote the catalogue entry to Munch's picture entitled *The Kiss*, "The fusion of two beings, the smaller of which, shaped like a carp, seems on the point of devouring the larger as is the habit of vermin, microbes, vampires, or women." But in the end he is closer to Ibsen than to

Strindberg and his repeated motif of mother and daughter shows a calm acceptance of destiny that Strindberg rejected.

Although Munch spent many of his formative years in Paris and Berlin (as Ibsen spent his in Italy) he remains an essentially Nordic artist, who perhaps cannot be fully understood by anyone who has not swallowed large gulps of northern air. For the interminable twilight of summer he invented a curious symbol, which I suppose was inspired by a sun obstinately refusing to set, but looks like a candle with a globe above it. It is in the background of a picture called *The Voice,* painted in 1893, and reappears, looking like an Egyptian hieroglyphic, in his latest works. The icy breath of a northern winter he conveyed in a series of superb landscapes, which must surely convince anyone of his greatness as a 'pure' painter.

In 1908 his overstretched nervous system collapsed, and he was confined to a clinic in Copenhagen. Writers on Munch maintain that he was not disturbed by this breakdown; but I find that it affected him profoundly. He seemed afraid that the symbols which had haunted him so long were like a dangerous magic, and might again upset his mental balance: so no more devouring women, no more whispering girls like white tents, no more summer nights. The greatest of his winter landscapes date from after his nervous collapse. And in these years an unpredictable thing happened. This man who had been a friend of the Symbolist poets in Paris, the least socially conscious of all groups, became passionately interested in the workers. In 1911 he painted a picture of snow shovellers which is perhaps the greatest of all attempts in this century to achieve what is known as socialist realism. The figures have the frontality which for Munch symbolised virility; they also have a look of weatherbeaten trees that have defied a hostile climate; and the whole is painted with vigorous pictorial freedom that is usually discouraged among realists in socialist countries.

Munch was undoubtedly the greatest painter of northern Europe; but it would be wrong to make too much of this geographical accident. He would have been a great painter anywhere, and in fact his pictorial aims were much closer to those of the main tradition of European art, from Giotto onwards, than were the aims of the Impressionists. Of all painters Giotto had the greatest gift of creating combinations of forms that seem totally and inevitably to embody a human relationship. Of course Munch's range was more limited, and his view of life less charitable; but his artistic aims were of the same order, and at his best he achieved them with an intensity that has rarely been equalled.

Edvard Munch (1863–1944)
by Knut Berg

This exhibition of the work of Edvard Munch, which is being shown in three of the chief art centres of Europe – Munich, London and Paris – is one of the most representative displays of paintings by the great Norwegian master to have been organised since 1945. On behalf of the Norwegian lenders I wish to express our gratitude for the collaboration of the three institutions showing the exhibition: the Haus der Kunst in Munich, the Arts Council of Great Britain in London, and the Musée National d'Art Moderne in Paris. It is a pleasure for us to have this opportunity of once again presenting the art of Edvard Munch to a wider European public.

Long recognised as one of the great pioneers of modern art, Munch seems more a European rather than a purely Norwegian figure. After his basic artistic education in the naturalistic tradition in Norway in the 1880s, his expressive and highly individual style developed in the following decades through contact with, above all, French and German art.

He first travelled abroad in 1885 when at the age of 22 he went to Paris for three weeks. The French Impressionists were a revelation to him, and after his return home it is easy to see how much more lightly and freely his brush moved over the canvas. The old masters in the Louvre made a strong impression on him; he was evidently much influenced by Rembrandt which may be seen from *The Sick Child* (1885–86), a painting which can in many ways be regarded as fundamental to his life's work.

Munch's first one-man exhibition in 1889 concludes the first period of his development. In that year he went abroad again with the aid of a state grant, and until he returned to Norway for good in 1909 he spent most of his time, except for summer holidays in Norway, in France and Germany.

Munch went first to stay in France where he remained for nearly three years. The nineties were a period of change in French art. In Paris, the meeting place for almost every trend and tendency in the art of the time, Munch was exposed to the most varied influences. His contact with the Neo-Impressionists appears at an early date in a picture such as *Rue Lafayette* (1891, No. 8); but his contact with the Symbolists and especially with Gauguin was of far greater importance. It provided the basis for his new style of simplified figure drawing, the use of line as an expressive element, and the emotive juxtaposition of large areas of uniform colour as in *Melancholy* (c.1891, No. 10). Here was a style capable of embodying the intense emotional life to which Munch sought to give expression in his art.

Munch sent mainly pictures of this period in response to the invitation of the revered Verein Berliner Künstler to hold an exhibition under their auspices in 1892.

The show raised a furore and was closed after a week. Controversy became acute, and split the Verein in two, a split which led subsequently to the formation of the Berliner Sezessioni. A wind of change was blowing through German art, and Munch became renowned as an exponent of contemporary radicalism.

Munch himself went to Berlin at the end of 1892, and from then until 1908 he stayed for long periods in Germany. In Berlin he became part of a cosmopolitan circle of writers, poets and philosophers. During the years until 1900 he was at work on *The Frieze of Life*, which is probably his most important work. It is not a frieze in the usual sense of forming a decorative unity. The component pictures are different in size and were painted in various techniques. There are several versions of most of them. The work is best described as a series of pictures united in content. It is a poem about life, love and death; hate and fear; the relations between the sexes; and woman as a daemonic power. The *Frieze* is one of the most passionate expressions of intimate emotional life in the whole history of art. The separate titles best indicate its content: *Puberty* (No. 16), *Attraction, The Kiss* (No. 12), *Desire, Jealousy* (No. 26), *The Vampire* (No. 22), *Ashes, Madonna* (No. 25), *Three Stages of Woman, Death in the Sick Room, The Dance of Life* (No. 33), etc. These were themes in which the painter never lost interest, and he returned to themes from the *Frieze* throughout his life. *The Dance of Life* (1899–1900, No. 33) is perhaps the work that best typifies his art at this period, both in emotional intensity and in the expressiveness of its technique.

The atmosphere of Berlin must have contributed to the development of his art at this period, but the effect of the summers he spent in Norway cannot be overlooked. The undulating shore line and great stone boulders of his beloved Åsgårdstrand on the Oslo Fjord had an indelible effect on his painting. Here he found a landscape which reflected the undulating lines of the Art Nouveau of this time, while from the luminous, poetic summer nights he drew the inspiration for his evocative palette.

Munch's first graphic work was also done in Berlin in 1894. Originally he was mainly interested in drypoint; however his real breakthrough as a draughtsman came in Paris in 1896. There he learnt to master lithography and also the difficult art of printing woodcuts. He was aided in this not only by the inspiration of the graphic work of French masters such as Toulouse-Lautrec, Redon, Carrière, Gauguin and others, but also by working with printers like Clot and Lemercier.

Graphic art soon became no less important to him than painting as a means of expressing emotions and ideas. In his woodcuts, especially those in colour, Munch was a pioneer; few have done as much as he to exploit the possibilities of this medium. Graphic art released new aspects of his talent. The professional crafts-manship involved in the handling of the copperplate, the lithographic stone, or the wood-block demanded a concentration that may explain why it was in graphic art that his ideas found, aesthetically speaking, perhaps their purest expression.

Munch's work of the 1890s is marked by intense, expressive colour, often predominantly dark in tone, undulating line and large areas of uniform colour. After the turn of the century he developed a freer, more lively style. The tones were brighter, he used clearer and purer colours, and his brushwork became expressive in itself. Sharp contrasts of colour were conveyed in powerful strokes, and his pictures revealed a new, more brutal expressiveness. One suspects a connection with the Fauves, but this problem, like that of Munch's influence on German Expressionism, still remains to be fully investigated. Munch's range of subject matter increases, the themes of the '90s are further developed, an element of the macabre appears. From this period comes the series of fine portraits of life size, powerful and monumental, but at the same time there also begins to emerge a more lyrical, painterly style. There are manifest in the mind and mood of the artist those tendencies which were to lead to his nervous collapse in 1908.

Munch spent about a year in a clinic in Copenhagen and in 1909, at the age of 45, returned to Norway where he lived until his death. It was as though he needed peace and quiet after the stormy years of constant travelling abroad. His chosen place of retirement was Kragerø, an idyllic village on the outer Oslo Fjord. Here Munch began work on the murals for the new ceremonial hall of Oslo University, his only major commission of this kind. In it he developed further the powerful, monumental style he had evolved at the beginning of the century. These murals also represent, however, a new departure in content. Their tone is lighter and more optimistic, and the huge sun in the centre panel, shining down upon the Norwegian coastal landscape, may serve to symbolise the mood of the artist's final period.

In 1916 Munch bought a large old villa at Ekely near Oslo. There he spent the rest of his days in retirement, visited only by a few close friends and his models. In spite of his seclusion, his work at this time showed a more outgoing attitude towards the world around him. He was less preoccupied with sounding the psychological depths, his art became more extrovert, his style freer and brighter. Large landscapes, scenes of workmen or more contemplative studies of models reveal his pleasure in the activity of painting. When he reverted to the themes of his younger days, the psychological intensity of his earlier years is missing.

Munch did not found a school. His importance for the development of modern painting was due primarily to his unconventional, direct and subjective handling of the medium. His directness, his rapid almost reckless spontaneity, and his honest way of saying what he had to say left a deep imprint upon the art of our time.

Some Quotations from Writings by Munch

A strong, bare arm, a sunburned, muscular neck – a young woman rests her head on his arching chest. She closes her eyes and listens with open, quivering lips to the words he whispers into her long flowing hair.

I would give form to this as I now see it, but envelop it in a blue haze. These two in that moment when they are no longer themselves but only one of thousands of links tying one generation to another generation. People should understand the sanctity of this moment and take off their hats as if they were in church.

I would make a number of such paintings.

No longer would interiors, people who only read and knit, be painted. There should rather be living people breathing and feeling, suffering and loving. I felt I have to do this. It would be so simple. The flesh would take on form and the colours come to life.

Impressions from a ballroom, New Year's Eve in St Cloud, 1889

I was walking along the road with two friends. The sun set. I felt a tinge of melancholy. Suddenly the sky became a bloody red.

I stopped and leaned against the railing, dead tired, and I looked at the flaming clouds that hung like blood and a sword over the blue-black fjord and the city.

My friends walked on. I stood there, trembling with fright. And I felt a loud, unending scream piercing nature.

Diary entry, dated 22.1.92, Nice

I give her the soft loveliness of the bright mid-summer night. On her hair, on her face, on her white robes shimmers gold.

I place her in front of the dreaming blue of the ocean with the snake-like, sinuous lines of the seashore.

Then she leaves him, who still does not understand but feels her disappear as in a dream.

He stands surrounded by blood-red flowers, in the cold blue of evening shadows.

He still does not fully understand how it happened.

But even if she totally disappears across the ocean, he feels how individual threads of hair from her have entwined themselves tightly around his heart.

On 'The Frieze of Life', c.1893 or 1894*

I painted impressions from my childhood – the blurred colours from the time – by painting the colours and lines and shapes I had seen in moments of emotion – I tried once again, as on a gramophone, to reawaken the vibrant emotions.

On 'The Frieze of Life', Oslo, 1925

*Heller, Reinhold. 'Edvard Munch and the Clarification of Life', *The Epstein Collection, Allen Memorial Art Museum Bulletin*, XXIX, no. 3, Spring 1972, Oberlin 1972.

Chronology

1863 Edvard Munch born in Løten, Norway on 12 December, son of the military doctor Christian Munch and his wife Laura Cathrine.

1868 The artist's mother dies of tuberculosis and her sister, Karen Bjølstad takes over the household.

1877 His sister Sophie dies of tuberculosis at the age of 15.

1879 Enters the Technical College with the intention of becoming an engineer.

1882–83 Paints under the direction of Christian Krohg. Attends Frits Thaulow's 'open-air academy' at Modum.

1885 First stay, of three weeks, in Paris. Begins *The Sick Child, The Morning After, Puberty*. Comes into contact with the Bohemian circle of naturalist painters and intellectuals in Christiania (Oslo) led by Hans Jaeger.

1889–90 Travels to Paris on a State scholarship. Lives in Neuilly and St. Cloud while he attends Léon Bonnat's art school. Sees work of the Neo-Impressionists, Van Gogh and Gauguin.

1892 Invited to exhibit at the Verein der Berliner Künstler. After a violent debate the exhibition is closed, and the scandal makes Munch's name famous in Germany.

1893 Frequents the Berlin circle of Richard Dehmel, the poet Stanislav Przybyzewski, Julius Meier-Graefe, August Strindberg, and the contributors to the journal *Pan*.

1894 Produces his first lithographs and etchings.

1896 Prints coloured lithographs and his first woodcuts at Auguste Clot's in Paris. Designs lithograph for the programme of *Peer Gynt* at the Théâtre de l'Œuvre.

1898–1901 Travels in Germany, Italy and France. Summers spent at his home in Åsgårdstrand. Twice rests in a sanatorium.

1906–07 Drafts decor designs for Max Reinhardt's productions of Ibsen's *Ghosts* and *Hedda Gabler*. Decorates the foyer of Reinhardt's Kammerspiele, Deutsches Theater in Berlin.

1908 Paints *Mason and Mechanic*, first of a series about modern industrial life. In the autumn suffers a nervous collapse and enters Dr. Daniel Jacobson's clinic in Copenhagen.

1909 Returns to Norway to live. Paints life-size portraits and landscapes. Begins designing murals for competition for the decoration of Oslo University Festival Hall.

1916 Buys the estate of Ekely in Skøyen outside Oslo. Oslo University unveils the murals which include *Sun Rising over the Fjord*.

1922 Paints murals for the canteen of the Freia Chocolate Factory.

1937 82 works by Munch are branded as degenerate by the Germans. Munch gives financial support to the young painter Ernst Wilhelm Nay.

1940 Refuses to have any contact with the German invaders or the Quisling government.

1944 Dies on 23 January at Ekely. Bequeaths to the Municipality of Oslo all of the work in his possession, including 1,000 paintings, 15,400 etchings, lithographs and woodcuts, 4,500 watercolours and drawings and six sculptures.

Major Exhibitions during Munch's lifetime

1889 Student's Association, Oslo

1892 Jeweler Tostrup's Building, Oslo

1892 Verein Berliner Künstler, Architektenhaus, Berlin

1892 Eduard Schulte, Düsseldorf and Cologne

1893 George Kleis, Copenhagen

1893 Victoria-Haus, Dresden

1893 Ugo Barroccio, Berlin

1894 Galerie Blanche, Stockholm

1895 Blomqvists Lokale, Oslo

1896 Salon des Indépendants, Paris

1896 'Salon de l'Art Nouveau', S. Bing, Paris

1897 Dioramalokalet, Oslo

1900 Dioramalokalet, Høsten, Oslo

1900 Dresdner Kunstsalon, Dresden

1902 Sezession, Berlin

1903 P. H. Beyer and Sohn, Leipzig

1903 Blomqvists Lokale, Oslo

1905 Galerie Manés, Prague

1906 Großherzogliches Museum, Weimar

1909 Blomqvists Lokale, Oslo

1909 Bergens Kunstforening, Bergen

1912 Moderne Galerie Thannhauser, Munich

1913 Salon Joël, Stockholm

1913 Konstnärshuset, Stockholm

1914 Galerie Fritz Gurlitt, Berlin

1918 Blomqvists Lokale, Oslo

1922 Kunsthaus, Zürich

1927 Städtische Kunsthalle, Mannheim

1927 Kronprinzen-Palais, Berlin

1927 Nasjonalgalleriet, Oslo

1929 Künstlervereinigung, Dresden

1936 The London Gallery, London (first London exhibition)

1937 Stedelijk Museum, Amsterdam

1944 Nationalmuseum, Stockholm and Kunstmuseum, Gothenberg

1951 'Edvard Munch, An Exhibition of Paintings, Etchings and Lithographs', The Arts Council of Great Britain, Brighton; Glasgow; Tate Gallery, London (This large retrospective first toured the United States and went subsequently to The Hague and Paris)

Selected Bibliography

A detailed bibliography is contained in the publication *Oslo Kommunes Kunstsamlinger* by H. B. Muller.

Allen Memorial Art Museum Bulletin, The Epstein Collection, XXIX, no. 3, Spring. Oberlin, Ohio 1972.

BENESCH, OTTO. *Edvard Munch*. Cologne and London 1960.

GAUGUIN, POLA. *Edvard Munch*. Oslo 1933 (New edition 1946).

GLASER, CURT. *Edvard Munch*. Berlin 1917 (New edition 1922).

HELLER, REINHOLD. *Edvard Munch : The Scream*. London 1973.

HODIN, J. P. *Edvard Munch. Der Genius des Nordens*. Stockholm 1948 (German edition Mainz 1963); *Edvard Munch*. London 1972.

KOKOSCHKA, OSKAR. *Der Expressionismus Edvard Munchs*. Vienna, Linz, Munich 1953.

LANGAARD, INGRID. *Edvard Munch. Modningsår*. Oslo 1960.

LANGAARD, JOHAN H. AND REVOLD, REIDAR. *Edvard Munch. A Year by Year Record of Edvard Munch's Life*. Oslo 1961; *Edvard Munch: The University Murals*. Oslo 1961; *Edvard Munch. Masterpieces from the Artist's Collection in the Munch Museum in Oslo*. Oslo 1964 (Norwegian edition Oslo 1963, German edition Stuttgart 1963).

MOEN, ARVE. *Edvard Munch: Age and Milieu. Graphic Art and Paintings*. Oslo 1956; *Edvard Munch: Woman and Eros. Graphic Art and Paintings*. Oslo 1957; *Edvard Munch: Nature and Animals. Graphic Art and Paintings*. Oslo 1958.

MULLER, H. B. *Oslo Kommunes Kunstsamlinger. Edvard Munch. A Bibliography*. Årbok 1946–1951. Covers 59 years of contributions up to 1950 and supplements Årbok 1952–59. Berlin 1960 (Norwegian edition Oslo 1951 and 1960).

MUNCH, EDVARD. *The Life Frieze* (published in connection with the Blomqvist Exhibition in Oslo). Oslo 1918.

PRZYBYSZEWSKI, STANLISAW; MEIER-GRAEFE, JULIUS; PASTOR, WILLY; SERVAES, FRANZ. *Das Werk des Edvard Munch*. Berlin 1894.

SCHIEFLER, GUSTAV. *Edvard Munchs Graphische Kunst*. Dresden 1923; *Edvard Munch. Das Graphische Werk* 1906–1926. Berlin 1928.

STENERSEN, ROLF. *Edvard Munch: Close-up of a Genius*. Oslo 1969 (originally published Stockholm 1944).

THIIS, JENS. *Edvard Munch's Kunst*. Bergen 1904–1907; *Edvard Munch og hans samtid*. Oslo 1933 (German edition Berlin 1934).

TIMM, WERNER. *The Graphic Art of Edvard Munch*. London 1969 (German editions Leipzig 1966 and Berlin 1972).

Oil Paintings

Works illustrated in black and white are marked with an asterisk, those in colour with a double asterisk.

In the measurements height precedes width.

All oil on canvas.

1 **Self-portrait** 1881
25 × 18 cm
Munch-Museet, Oslo

2 **Girl Kindling the Stove** 1883
96·5 × 66 cm
Lent by F. Lorentzen

3 **Morning, Girl at the Bed Side** 1884
96·5 × 103·5 cm
Rasmus Meyer Collection, Bergen

4 **Tête-à-Tête** 1885*
65·5 × 75·5 cm
Munch-Museet, Oslo

5 **Girl Playing the Piano** 1886
36 × 31·5 cm
Munch-Museet, Oslo

6 **The Painter Thorvald Torgersen** 1886
100 × 68 cm
Munch-Museet, Oslo

7 **Military Band on Karl Johan Street, Oslo** 1889**
102 × 141·5 cm
Kunsthaus, Zürich

8 **Rue Lafayette** 1891*
92 × 73 cm
Nasjonalgalleriet, Oslo

9 **Spring Day on Karl Johan Street, Oslo** 1891
80 × 100 cm
Billedgalleri, Bergen

10 **Melancholy (The Yellow Boat)** 1891/93*
65 × 96 cm
Nasjonalgalleriet, Oslo

11 **Portrait of Inger, the Artist's Sister** 1892*
172 × 122·5 cm
Nasjonalgalleriet, Oslo

12 **The Kiss** 1892
100 × 80·5 cm
Munch-Museet, Oslo

13 **Evening on Karl Johan Street, Oslo** 1892
84·5 × 121 cm
Rasmus Meyer Collection, Bergen

14 **Ludwig Meyer** 1892
212·5 × 106 cm
Tröndelag Kunstgalleri, Trondheim

15 **August Strindberg** 1892
120 × 90 cm
Moderna Museet, Stockholm

16 **Puberty** c.1893*
150 × 112 cm
Munch-Museet, Oslo

17 **Starry Night** 1893
135 × 140 cm
Private Collection

18 **Dagny Juell Przybyszewska** 1893*
148·5 × 99·5 cm
Munch-Museet, Oslo

19 **Moonlight** 1893*
140·5 × 135 cm
Nasjonalgalleriet, Oslo

20 **The Scream** 1893**
91 × 73·5 cm
Nasjonalgalleriet, Oslo

21 **The Hands** 1893
89 × 76·5 cm
Munch-Museet, Oslo

22 **Vampire** c.1894*
100 × 110 cm
Private Collection, Norway

23 **Anxiety** 1894**
94 × 74 cm
Munch-Museet, Oslo

24 **The Day After** 1894/95*
115 × 152 cm
Nasjonalgalleriet, Oslo

25 **Madonna** 1894/95★★
91 × 70·5 cm
Nasjonalgalleriet, Oslo

26 **Jealousy** 1894/95★
67 × 100 cm
Rasmus Meyer Collection, Bergen

27 **The Voice** 1895★★
88 × 110 cm
Munch-Museet, Oslo

28 **Female Nude** 1896
64·5 × 48·5 cm
Rasmus Meyer Collection, Bergen

29 **Heritage** 1897/99
141 × 120 cm
Munch-Museet, Oslo

30 **Female Nude with Red Hair**
1892/1902
120 × 49·5 cm
Munch-Museet, Oslo

31 **The Virginia Creeper** 1898★
120 × 120 cm
Munch-Museet, Oslo

32 **Melancholy (Laura)** 1899
110 × 126 cm
Munch-Museet, Oslo

33 **The Dance of Life** 1899/1900★★
125·5 × 190·5
Nasjonalgalleriet, Oslo

34 **Train Smoke** c.1900
85 × 109 cm
Munch-Museet, Oslo

35 **Girls on a Jetty** c.1900
83·5 × 128·5 cm
Kunsthalle, Hamburg

36 **The Dance on the Shore** 1900/02★★
95·5 × 98·5 cm
Národní Galerie, Prague

37 **Consul Christen Sandberg** 1901
215 × 147 cm
Munch-Museet, Oslo

38 **Road in Åsgårdstrand** 1902★
114 × 88 cm
Schwarz-von Spreckelsen Collection,
Basel

39 **The Apple Tree** c.1902
75 × 88 cm
Hudtwalcker Collection

40 **The Beast (Female Nude half
length)** c.1902
94·7 × 63·5 cm
Niedersächsisches Landesmuseum,
Städtische Galerie, Hanover

41 **The Forest** 1903
82 × 81 cm
Munch-Museet, Oslo

42 **The Boch Family** 1903
197 × 122 cm
Thielska Galleriet, Stockholm

43 **Four Girls in Åsgårdstrand**
1904/05
87 × 111 cm
Munch-Museet, Oslo

44 **Heritage** 1905
120 × 100 cm
Munch-Museet, Oslo

45 **Elisabeth Förster-Nietzsche** 1905
115 × 80 cm
Munch-Museet, Oslo

46 **Self-portrait with Brushes** 1905
197 × 91·5 cm
Munch-Museet, Oslo

47 **Self-portrait with Wine Bottle**
1906★★
110·5 × 120·5 cm
Munch-Museet, Oslo

48 **Thüringen Landscape (Melting
Snow near Elgersburg)** 1906★
71 × 91 cm
Von der Heydt-Museum, Wuppertal

49 **Consolation** 1907
90 × 109 cm
Munch-Museet, Oslo

50 **Death of Marat** 1907★
151 × 148 cm
Munch-Museet, Oslo

51 **Amor and Psyche** 1907
119 × 99 cm
Munch-Museet, Oslo

52 **Nude at the Bed Side** 1907
120 × 121 cm
Munch-Museet, Oslo

53 **The Harbour at Lübeck** 1907
80·5 × 97·5 cm
Kunsthaus, Zürich

54 **Men Bathing** 1907/08
(Middle panel of a triptych)
206 × 227 cm
Ateneumin Taidemuseo, Helsinki

55 **Adam and Eve under the Apple Tree** 1908
130·5 × 202 cm
Munch-Museet, Oslo

56 **Dr. Daniel Jacobson** 1909*
204 × 112 cm
Munch-Museet, Oslo

57 **Self-portrait in a Blue Suit** 1909
100 × 100 cm
Rasmus Meyer Collection, Bergen

58 **Children in the Street** 1910
92 × 100 cm
Munch-Museet, Oslo

59 **The House by the Sea** 1910
92 × 116 cm
Munch-Museet, Oslo

60 **The Murderer** 1911
94·5 × 154 cm
Munch-Museet, Oslo

61 **Couple by the Shore** 1911*
81 × 121 cm
Munch-Museet, Oslo

62 **Galloping Horse** 1912*
148 × 120 cm
Munch-Museet, Oslo

63 **Workers Returning Home** 1912*
200 × 227 cm
Munch-Museet, Oslo

64 **The Tree Trunk** 1912*
131 × 160 cm
Munch-Museet, Oslo

65 **Jealousy (Passion)** 1913*
85 × 130 cm
Lent by O. Hudtwalcker, Barcelona

66 **Self-portrait, the Night-Wanderer** c.1920
90 × 68 cm
Munch-Museet, Oslo

67 **Starry Night** 1923*
120·5 × 100 cm
Munch-Museet, Oslo

68 **The Sick Child** 1927*
117 × 116 cm
Munch-Museet, Oslo

69 **Seated Model** 1928
136·5 × 115·5 cm
Munch-Museet, Oslo

70 **Nude by the Wicker Chair** 1929**
122·5 × 100 cm
Munch-Museet, Oslo

71 **Henriette Olsen** 1932
203 × 95 cm
Munch-Museet, Oslo

72 **Two Women by the Shore** 1935
80 × 83 cm
Munch-Museet, Oslo

73 **Self-portrait between Bed and Clock** 1940/42**
149·5 × 120·5 cm
Munch-Museet, Oslo

Watercolours, Pastels and Drawings

(Unless otherwise specified all works belong to the Munch-Museet, Oslo)

74 **At the Wine Merchant's** 1890
Pastel, 506 × 668 mm
Norske Selskab, Oslo

75 **Consolation** 1893/94
Charcoal, 479 × 630 mm

76 **The Hands** 1893/94*
Oil, gouache and charcoal,
672 × 452 mm

77 **The Kiss** 1894/95
Pencil, 189 × 289 mm

78 **The Maiden and the Heart** c.1896*
Crayon, 620 × 477 mm

79 **To the Forest** 1896
Pencil and watercolour, 322 × 174 mm

80 **Death of Omega** 1896
Charcoal, ink and pencil,
339 × 504 mm

81 **Seated Model** 1896*
Charcoal, pencil and watercolour,
620 × 477 mm

82 **Self-portrait with Lyre** 1897/98*
Pencil, ink, watercolour and gouache,
685 × 525 mm

83 **Sketch for Ibsen's** *Hedda Gabler*
1907*
(produced by Max Reinhardt's
Kammerspiele)
Watercolour and pencil, 575 × 455 mm

84 **Nude Model at the Window** 1907/08
Charcoal, watercolour and gouache,
609 × 494 mm

85 **Burlesque Scene (Men and Beasts)**
1908
Crayon, 382 × 571 mm

86 **Moonrise** 1908
Crayon, 255 × 480 mm

87 **The Spring** 1909/10
Watercolour and coloured crayon,
564 × 780 mm

88 **Cliffs by Kragerø** c.1910
Charcoal and watercolour over pencil,
488 × 605 mm

89 **The House on the Cliff** c.1910
Charcoal, pencil and watercolour,
474 × 607 mm

90 **Standing Woman in Room**
after 1912*
Charcoal and watercolour, 591 × 782 mm

91 **Self-portrait** 1916
Charcoal, 600 × 600 mm

92 **Workers on the Way Home (Eureka)**
after 1916
Charcoal and watercolour, 570 × 779 mm

93 **Self-portrait (After the Spanish
Flu)** 1920*
Crayon, 430 × 610 mm

94 **Girls on the Shore** c.1920
Pencil and watercolour, 238 × 289 mm

95 **Model in Dressing Gown** c.1920*
Charcoal and gouache, 981 × 608 mm

96 **Standing Model with Loosened
Hair** c.1920
Crayon, 905 × 530 mm

97 **Lady with a Blue Hat** after 1920
Watercolour, 665 × 520 mm

98 **Woman's Head (Portrait Study)**
after 1920
Watercolour, 292 × 228 mm

99 **Kneeling Nude Model** 1921
Watercolour, 354 × 510 mm

100 **Nude Model Undressing** c.1925
Coloured crayon and watercolour,
353 × 257 mm

101 **Birgitte Prestø** c.1930
Watercolour, 348 × 248 mm

102 **Self-portrait as Seated Nude**
1933/34*
Pencil and watercolour, 700 × 862 mm

103 **Young Men and Women on the Shore** c.1935
Watercolour and coloured crayon, 700 × 862 mm

104 **Self-portrait at 2 a.m.** after 1940★
Oil on paper, 515 × 645 mm

105 **Self-portrait with stick of pastel** 1943
Pastel, 800 × 600 mm

Graphic Works

ETCHINGS

106 **Death and the Maiden** 1894★
Drypoint, 305 × 220 mm
Schiefler No. 3

107 **The Sick Child** 1894
Drypoint with roller, 387 × 293 mm
Schiefler No. 7

108 **Tête-à-Tête** 1895
Drypoint and etching, 218 × 328 mm
Schiefler No. 12

109 **Moonlight (Night in St Cloud)** 1895★
Drypoint and aquatint, 310 × 254 mm
Schiefler No. 13

110 **The Day After** 1895
Drypoint and aquatint, 206 × 296 mm
Schiefler No. 15

111 **Lovers on the Shore (Attraction II)** 1895★
Drypoint and etching, 215 × 315 mm
Schiefler No. 18

112 **Summer Night (The Voice)** 1895
Drypoint and aquatint, 237 × 314 mm
Schiefler No. 19

113 **Two People (The Lonely Ones)** 1895
Drypoint, 155 × 214 mm
Schiefler No. 20

114 **Woman I (The Sphinx)** 1895
Drypoint and aquatint, 315 × 260 mm
Schiefler No. 21A

115 **Woman II (The Sphinx)** 1895★
Drypoint and aquatint, 298 × 347 mm
Schiefler No. 21B

116 **The Kiss** 1895★
Drypoint and aquatint, 345 × 278 mm
Schiefler No. 22

117 **Stephane Mallarmé** 1896
Drypoint, 198 × 160 mm

118 **Nude Girl** 1896
Mezzotint, 145 × 127·5 mm
Schiefler No. 39

119 **Nude Girl** 1896
Mezzotint, 146 × 128·5 mm
Schiefler No. 40

120 **Reclining Female Nude** 1896
Etching and mezzotint, 216 × 290 mm
Schiefler No. 41

121 **Young Girl on the Shore** 1896★
Coloured mezzotint, 287 × 218 mm
Schiefler No. 42

122 **Lovers in the Waves** 1896
Mezzotint, 216 × 288 mm
Schiefler No. 43

123 **Two Maidens and a Skeleton** 1896
Drypoint, 315 × 429 mm
Schiefler No. 44

124 **The Maiden and the Heart** 1896
Drypoint and etching, 243 × 345 mm
Schiefler No. 48

125 **Night Street Scene** 1897
Drypoint, 237 × 297 mm
Schiefler No. 84
Private Collection

126 **Youths Bathing** 1897★
Mezzotint, 300 × 239 mm
Schiefler No. 85

127 **Sigbjørn Obstfelder** 1897
Drypoint and etching, 179 × 137 mm
Schiefler No. 88

128 **Helge Rode** 1898
Drypoint, 276 × 208 mm
Schiefler No. 103

129 **The Dead Mother and the Child** 1901★
Etching and aquatint, 322 × 494 mm
Schiefler No. 140

130 **Potsdamer Platz** 1902
Drypoint and aquatint, 238 × 297 mm
Schiefler No. 156

131 **Puberty** 1902
Etching, 198 × 160 mm
Schiefler No. 164

132 **The Big Fish** 1902★
Etching, 128 × 176 mm
Schiefler No. 165

133 **Dr Linde's House** 1902★
Etching, 492 × 645 mm
Schiefler No. 187

134 **Dr Linde's Garden by Night** 1902
Drypoint and aquatint, 495 × 645 mm
Schiefler No. 189

135 **Lübeck** 1902
Etching, 495 × 643 mm
Schiefler No. 195

136 **The Oak** 1903
Etching, 642 × 496 mm
Schiefler No. 196

137 **Girls on the Jetty** 1903★
Drypoint and aquatint, 188 × 264 mm
Schiefler No. 200

138 **Roulette** 1903
Etching, 270 × 443 mm
Schiefler No. 202

139 **The Nurse (Miss Schacke)** 1908/09★
Drypoint, 205 × 152 mm
Schiefler No. 269

140 **The Rag Picker** 1908/09
Etching, 600 × 440 mm
Schiefler No. 272

141 **Female Nude Standing** 1913/14
Etching, 492 × 245 mm
Schiefler No. 393

142 **The Bite** 1913/14★
Etching, 197 × 276 mm
Schiefler No. 396

143 **The Cat** 1913
Etching, 240 × 315 mm
Schiefler No. 397

144 **Two People** 1913
Drypoint, 178 × 239 mm
Schiefler No. 398

145 **Lovers** 1913
Etching, 198 × 280 mm
Schiefler No. 399

146 **Ashes** 1913
Etching, 200 × 278 mm
Schiefler No. 400

147 **Galloping Horse** 1915
Etching, 380 × 329 mm
Schiefler No. 431

LITHOGRAPHS

148 **Self-portrait with Skeleton Arm**
1895*
Lithograph, ink and crayon on stone,
460 × 322 mm
Schiefler No. 31

149 **The Scream** 1895*
Lithograph, 355 × 254 mm
Schiefler No. 32
Print Collection, Staatsgalerie,
Stuttgart

150 **Madonna** 1895/1902*
Coloured lithograph, ink and crayon
on stone
Sheet A: 605 × 442 mm
Sheet B: 440 × 442 mm
Schiefler No. 33

151 **Vampire** 1895**
Coloured lithograph and woodcut,
388 × 552 mm
Schiefler No. 34

152 **The Hands (Desire)** 1895
Lithograph, 480 × 305 mm
Schiefler No. 35

153 **The Alley (Carmen)** 1895
Lithograph, 470 × 305 mm
Schiefler No. 36

154 **In the Hospital** 1896
Lithograph, 330 × 540 mm
Schiefler No. 55

155 **In the Women's Hospital** 1896*
Lithograph, 350 × 490 mm
Schiefler No. 56

156 **Jealousy** 1896
Lithograph, 465 × 570 mm
Schiefler No. 58

157 **The Sick Child** 1896*
Lithograph, 421 × 565 mm
Schiefler No. 59

158 **Anxiety** 1896
Coloured lithograph, 420 × 385 mm
Schiefler No. 61

159 **Attraction I** 1896
Lithograph, 472 × 355 mm
Schiefler No. 65

160 **Attraction II** 1896
Lithograph, 395 × 625 mm
Schiefler No. 66

161 **Separation I** 1896*
Lithograph with watercolour,
488 × 585 mm
Schiefler No. 67
Rasmus Meyer Collection, Bergen

162 **Separation II** 1896
Coloured lithograph, 415 × 630 mm
Schiefler No. 68

163 **Lovers in the Waves** 1896*
Lithograph, 322 × 430 mm
Schiefler No. 71

164 **At the Deathbed** 1896*
Lithograph, 400 × 505 mm
Schiefler No. 72

165 **Death in the Sick Chamber** 1896
Lithograph, 400 × 540 mm
Schiefler No. 73

166 **Hans Jaeger** 1896*
Lithograph, 460 × 330 mm
Schiefler No. 76

167 **August Strindberg** 1896
Lithograph, 610 × 460 mm
Schiefler No. 77

168 **Funeral March** 1896
Lithograph, 555 × 370 mm
Schiefler No. 94

169 **Stanislav Przybyszewski** 1898
Lithograph, 542 × 441 mm
Schiefler No. 105

170 **Burlesque Lovers** 1898
Lithograph, 300 × 365 mm
Schiefler No. 106

171 **Desire** 1898
Lithograph, 293 × 398 mm
Schiefler No. 108

172 **Ashes** 1899
Lithograph, 353 × 454 mm
Schiefler No. 120
Nasjonalgalleriet, Oslo

173 **Homage to the Party** 1899
Lithograph, 405 × 530 mm
Schiefler No. 121

174 **Woman (The Sphinx)** 1899
Lithograph, 462 × 592 mm
Schiefler No. 122

175 **Harpy** 1900
Lithograph, 365 × 320 mm
Schiefler No. 137

176 **Holger Drachmann** 1901
Lithograph, 589 × 452 mm
Schiefler No. 141

177 **Nude with Red Hair (Sin)** 1901
Coloured lithograph, 495 × 399 mm
Schiefler No. 142

178 **Male Model** 1902
Lithograph, 483 × 365 mm
Schiefler No. 169

179 **Henrik Ibsen in the Café of the
Grand Hotel** 1902*
Lithograph, 430 × 590 mm
Schiefler No. 171

180 **The Swamp** 1903
Lithograph, 260 × 495 mm
Schiefler No. 205

181 **The Violin Concert** 1903
(Bella Edwards and Eva Mudocci)
Lithograph, 480 × 540 mm
Schiefler No. 211

182 **Madonna (The Brooch)** 1903*
Lithograph, 600 × 460 mm
Schiefler No. 212

183 **Salome** 1903
(Eva Mudocci and Munch)
Lithograph, 405 × 305 mm
Schiefler No. 213

184 **Self-portrait with Cigarette** 1909
Lithograph, 560 × 455 mm
Schiefler No. 282

185 **Starry Night (Romersholm)** c.1920
Lithograph, 400 × 360 mm

WOODCUTS

186 **Anxiety** 1896
Coloured woodcut, 460 × 377 mm
Schiefler No. 62

187 **Man's Head in Woman's Hair** 1896
Coloured woodcut, 546 × 381 mm
Schiefler No. 80

188 **Moonlight** 1896
Coloured woodcut, 412 × 467 mm
Schiefler No. 81

189 **Evening (Melancholy)** 1896*
Coloured woodcut, 376 × 455 mm
Schiefler No. 82

190 **Summer Night (The Voice)** 1896
Coloured woodcut, 378 × 560 mm
Schiefler No. 83

191 **In Man's Brain** 1897
Woodcut, 372 × 567 mm
Schiefler No. 98

192 **To the Forest** 1897
Coloured woodcut, 500 × 570 mm
Schiefler No. 100

193 **The Kiss** 1897/98
Woodcut, 591 × 457 mm
Schiefler No. 102A

194 **The Kiss** 1898*
Woodcut, 410 × 466 mm
Schiefler No. 102D

195 **Fertility** 1898*
Woodcut, 425 × 517 mm
Schiefler No. 110

196 **The Flower of Grief** 1898
Coloured woodcut, 465 × 330 mm
Schiefler No. 114

197 **Melancholy** 1898
Coloured woodcut, 333 × 422 mm
Schiefler No. 116

198 **Women on the Beach** 1898*
Coloured woodcut, 455 × 508 mm
Schiefler No. 117

199 **Winter Landscape in the Snow**
1898
Woodcut, 318 × 458 mm
Schiefler No. 118

200 **Coastal Landscape (The Tree Stump)** 1899
Coloured woodcut, 372 × 572 mm
Schiefler No. 125

201 **Man Bathing** 1899
Coloured woodcut, 440 × 440 mm
Schiefler No. 126

202 **Youths Bathing** 1899
Woodcut, 359 × 440 mm
Schiefler No. 127

203 **The Water Nymph** 1899
Woodcut, 425 × 518 mm
Schiefler No. 128

204 **Head of a Girl by the Shore** 1899*
Coloured woodcut, 475 × 413 mm
Schiefler No. 129

205 **The Fat Whore** 1899
Coloured woodcut, 250 × 200 mm
Schiefler No. 131

206 **Man and Woman** 1899
Woodcut, 420 × 510 mm
Schiefler No. 132

207 **Two People (The Lonely Ones)** 1899**
Coloured woodcut, 395 × 530 mm
Schiefler No. 133

208 **The Heart** 1899
Coloured woodcut, 252 × 184 mm
Schiefler No. 134

209 **Encounter in Space** 1899
Coloured woodcut, 181 × 251 mm
Schiefler No. 135

210 **Evening (Melancholy III)** 1901
Coloured woodcut, 385 × 450 mm
Schiefler No. 144

211 **Old Man Praying** 1902
Woodcut, 458 × 325 mm
Schiefler No. 173

212 **The Apple Tree** 1902
Woodcut, 350 × 439 mm
Schiefler No. 175

213 **Head to Head** 1905*
Coloured woodcut, 400 × 540 mm
Schiefler No. 230

214 **Self-portrait** 1911
Woodcut, 540 × 350 mm
Schiefler No. 352

215 **Self-portrait** c.1915
Woodcut, 440 × 353 mm

216 **Sunbathing (Woman on the Rock)** 1915*
Coloured woodcut, 351 × 566 mm
Schiefler No. 440

217 **Lovers in the Pine Forest** 1915
Coloured woodcut, 320 × 600 mm
Schiefler No. 442

218 **Kiss on the Hair** 1915
Woodcut, 158 × 170 mm
Schiefler No. 443

219 **Girls on the Jetty** 1920*
Woodcut and coloured lithograph, 498 × 428 mm
Schiefler No. 488

220 **Trial by Fire** 1927/31
Woodcut, 458 × 373 mm

221 **Gothic Maiden (Birgitte Perstø)** 1930*
Woodcut, 600 × 320 mm

Edvard Munch, 1912

Munch with sister Laura (standing) in Åsgårdstrand, 1889

Munch in the Kornhaug Sanatorium, 1899

Munch with pencil and palette, left hand in bandage, c.1902

Munch in Kragerø, *c.*1910

Munch (at left) with friends near Fredensborgsvelen, 1915

Munch sitting in his studio in Ekely, 1943

7 Military Band on Karl Johan Street, Oslo 1899

20 The Scream 1893

23 Anxiety 1894

25 Madonna 1894/95

27 The Voice 1895

33 The Dance of Life 1899/1900

47 Self-portrait with Wine Bottle 1906

70 Nude by the Wicker Chair 1929

73 Self-portrait between Bed and Clock 1940/42

151 Vampire 1895

207 Two People (The Lonely Ones) 1899

10 Melancho'

11 Portrait of Inger (The Artist's Sister) 1892

18 Dagny Juell Przbyszewski 1893

16 Puberty *c.*1893

24 The Day After 1894/95

22 Vampire *c.*1894

38 Road in Åsgårdstrand 1902

19 Moonlight 1893

26 Jealousy 1894/95

31 The Virginia Creeper 1898

56 Dr Daniel Jacobson
1909

50 The Death of Marat 1907

48 Thüringen Landscape (Melting Snow near Elgersburg) 1906

64 The Tree Trunk 1912

62 Galloping Horse 1912

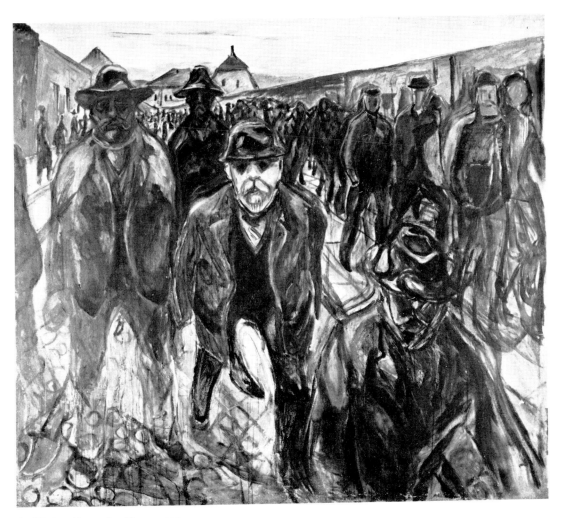

63 Workers Returning Home 1912

61 Couple by the Shore 1911

65 Jealousy (Passion) 1913

68 The Sick Child 1927

67 Starry Night 1923

82 Self-portrait with Lyre 1897/98

76 The Hands 1893/94

81 Seated Model 1896

106 Death and the Maiden 1894

109 Moonlight (Night in St Cloud) 1895

78 The Maiden and the Heart c.1896

111 Lovers on the Shore (Attraction II) 1895

116 The Kiss 1895

121 Young Girl on the Shore 1896

132 The Big Fish 1902

148 Self-portrait with Skeleton Arm 1895

150 Madonna 1895/1902

115 Woman II (The Sphinx) 1895

126 Youths Bathing 1897

164 At the Deathbed 1896

155 In the Women's Hospital 1896

149 The Scream 1895

204 Head of a Girl by the Shore 1899

198 Women on the Beach 1898

195 Fertility 1898

194 The Kiss 1898

142 The Bite 1913/14

182 Madonna (The Brooch) 1903

166 Hans Jaeger 1896

163 Lovers in the Waves 1896

213 Head to Head 1905

137 Girls on the Jetty 1903

133 Dr Linde's House 1902

129 The Dead Mother and the Child 1901

139 The Nurse (Miss Schacke) 1908/09

157 The Sick Child 1896

90 Standing Woman in Room *after* 1912

179 Henrik Ibsen in the Café of the Grand Hotel 1902

83 Sketch for Ibsen's *Hedda Gabler* 1907

161 Separation I 1896

189 Evening (Melancholy) 1896

219 Girls on the Jetty 1920

221 Gothic Maiden (Birgitte Perstø) 1930

216 Sunbathing (Woman on the Rock) 1915

102 Self-portrait as Seated Nude 1933/34

95 Model in Dressing Gown c.1920

93 Self-portrait (After the Spanish Flu) 1920

104 Self-portrait at 2 a.m. *after* 1940